THE PHILLIP KEVEREN SERIES   PIANO SOLO

BEST PIANO SOLOS

— PIANO LEVEL —
LATE INTERMEDIATE/EARLY ADVANCED

ISBN 978-1-4584-2099-2

HAL•LEONARD®
CORPORATION
7777 W. BLUEMOUND RD. P.O. BOX 13819 MILWAUKEE, WI 53213

For all works contained herein:
Unauthorized copying, arranging, adapting, recording, Internet posting, public performance,
or other distribution of the printed music in this publication is an infringement of copyright.
Infringers are liable under the law.

Visit Hal Leonard Online at
www.halleonard.com

Visit Phillip at
www.phillipkeveren.com

PREFACE

The Phillip Keveren Series launched in the year 2000 with a book entitled *The Celtic Collection*. A dozen years later, this folio marks the 82nd book in this publishing venture!

As they say, time flies when you are having fun—and writing these books has certainly been a great pleasure and privilege. I have really enjoyed meeting pianists from around the world, whether in person or via the Internet. Your kind messages of encouragement and suggestions for future books have meant a lot to me.

This collection features popular songs from the 1930s through the 2000s. Every one of these titles has been an enormously successful song, definitely the cream of the crop in the popular music idiom.

I hope you enjoy this "baker's dozen" of arrangements for the instrument we all love—the piano!

Sincerely,

Phillip Keveren

BIOGRAPHY

Phillip Keveren, a multi-talented keyboard artist and composer, has composed original works in a variety of genres from piano solo to symphonic orchestra. Mr. Keveren gives frequent concerts and workshops for teachers and their students in the United States, Canada, Europe, and Asia. Mr. Keveren holds a B.M. in composition from California State University Northridge and a M.M. in composition from the University of Southern California.

CONTENTS

4   **CAN'T HELP FALLING IN LOVE**

8   **DON'T KNOW WHY**

12   **FIELDS OF GOLD**

15   **FLY ME TO THE MOON (IN OTHER WORDS)**

18   **HALLELUJAH**

22   **I'LL BE SEEING YOU**

28   **KILLING ME SOFTLY WITH HIS SONG**

32   **MEMORY**

36   **OL' MAN RIVER**

38   **RIGHT HERE WAITING**

25   **THREE COINS IN THE FOUNTAIN**

42   **TIME IN A BOTTLE**

46   **WHERE DO I BEGIN (LOVE THEME)**

CAN'T HELP FALLING IN LOVE

from the Paramount Picture BLUE HAWAII

Words and Music by GEORGE DAVID WEISS,
HUGO PERETTI and LUIGI CREATORE
Arranged by Phillip Keveren

Copyright © 1961; Renewed 1989 Gladys Music (ASCAP)
This arrangement Copyright © 2012 Gladys Music
Published by Gladys Music for the world
Administered by BMG Chrysalis for the United States and Canada
International Copyright Secured   All Rights Reserved

DON'T KNOW WHY

Words and Music by
JESSE HARRIS
Arranged by Phillip Keveren

Copyright © 2002 Sony/ATV Music Publishing LLC and Beanly Songs
This arrangement Copyright © 2012 Sony/ATV Music Publishing LLC and Beanly Songs
All Rights Administered by Sony/ATV Music Publishing LLC, 8 Music Square West, Nashville, TN 37203
International Copyright Secured   All Rights Reserved

FIELDS OF GOLD

Music and Lyrics by
STING
Arranged by Phillip Keveren

© 1993 STEERPIKE LTD.
This arrangement © 2012 STEERPIKE LTD.
Administered by EMI MUSIC PUBLISHING LIMITED
All Rights Reserved   International Copyright Secured   Used by Permission

FLY ME TO THE MOON
(In Other Words)

Words and Music by
BART HOWARD
Arranged by Phillip Keveren

TRO - © Copyright 1954 (Renewed) Hampshire House Publishing Corp., New York, NY
This arrangement TRO – © Copyright 2012 Hampshire House Publishing Corp.
International Copyright Secured
All Rights Reserved Including Public Performance For Profit
Used by Permission

HALLELUJAH

Words and Music by
LEONARD COHEN
Arranged by Phillip Keveren

Copyright © 1995 Sony/ATV Music Publishing LLC
This arrangement Copyright © 2012 Sony/ATV Music Publishing LLC
All Rights Administered by Sony/ATV Music Publishing LLC, 8 Music Square West, Nashville, TN 37203
International Copyright Secured   All Rights Reserved

I'LL BE SEEING YOU
from RIGHT THIS WAY

Written by IRVING KAHAL
and SAMMY FAIN
Arranged by Phillip Keveren

© 1938 (Renewed 1966, 1994) THE NEW IRVING KAHAL MUSIC (ASCAP)/Administered by BUG MUSIC and FAIN MUSIC CO.
This arrangement © 2012 THE NEW IRVING KAHAL MUSIC (ASCAP)/Administered by BUG MUSIC and FAIN MUSIC CO.
All Rights Reserved   Used by Permission

THREE COINS IN THE FOUNTAIN

from THREE COINS IN THE FOUNTAIN

Words by SAMMY CAHN
Music by JULE STYNE
Arranged by Phillip Keveren

Copyright © 1954 by Producers Music Publishing Co. and Cahn Music Company
Copyright Renewed
This arrangement Copyright © 2012 by Producers Music Publishing Co. and Cahn Music Company
All Rights for Producers Music Publishing Co. Administered by Chappell & Co.
International Copyright Secured   All Rights Reserved

KILLING ME SOFTLY WITH HIS SONG

Words by NORMAN GIMBEL
Music by CHARLES FOX
Arranged by Phillip Keveren

Flowing (♩ = 100)

With pedal

Copyright © 1972 Rodali Music and Words West LLC (P.O. Box 15187, Beverly Hills, CA 90209 USA)
Copyright Renewed
This arrangement Copyright © 2012 Rodali Music and Words West LLC
International Copyright Secured   All Rights Reserved

MEMORY
from CATS

Music by ANDREW LLOYD WEBBER
Text by TREVOR NUNN after T.S. ELIOT
Arranged by Phillip Keveren

Music Copyright © 1981 Andrew Lloyd Webber licensed to The Really Useful Group Ltd.
Text Copyright © 1981 Trevor Nunn and Set Copyrights Ltd.
This arrangement Copyright © 2012 Andrew Lloyd Webber licensed to The Really Useful Group Ltd.
All Rights in the text Controlled by Faber and Faber Ltd. and Administered for the United States and Canada by R&H Music Co.
International Copyright Secured   All Rights Reserved

OL' MAN RIVER
from SHOW BOAT

Lyrics by OSCAR HAMMERSTEIN II
Music by JEROME KERN
Arranged by Phillip Keveren

Copyright © 1927 UNIVERSAL - POLYGRAM INTERNATIONAL PUBLISHING, INC.
Copyright Renewed
This arrangement Copyright © 2012 UNIVERSAL - POLYGRAM INTERNATIONAL PUBLISHING, INC.
All Rights Reserved   Used by Permission

RIGHT HERE WAITING

Words and Music by
RICHARD MARX
Arranged by Phillip Keveren

Tenderly (♩ = 88–92)

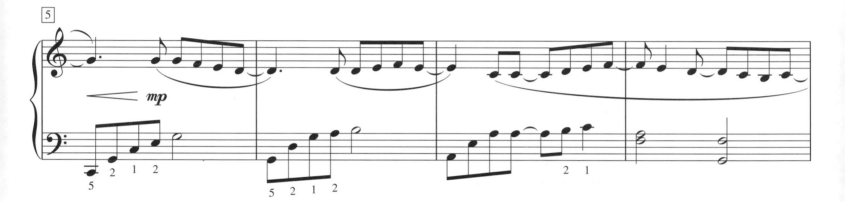

Copyright © 1989 Chrysalis Music
This arrangement Copyright © 2012 Chrysalis Music
All Rights Administered by BMG Rights Management (US) LLC
All Rights Reserved   Used by Permission

cantabile

TIME IN A BOTTLE

Words and Music by
JIM CROCE
Arranged by Phillip Keveren

With pedal

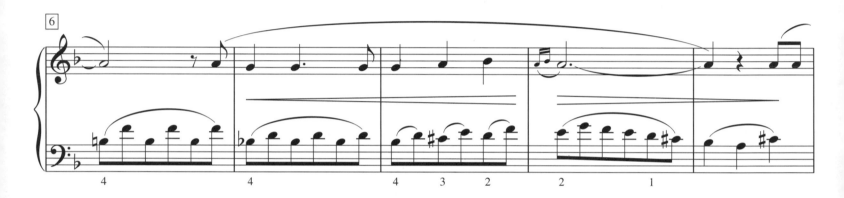

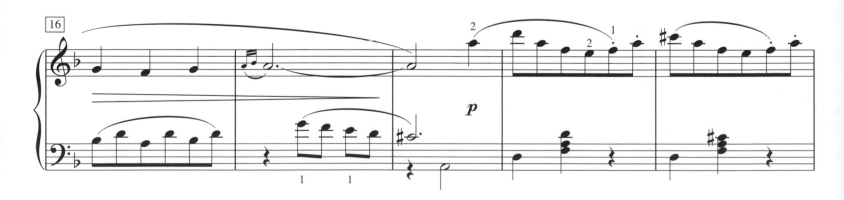

© 1971 (Renewed 1999) TIME IN A BOTTLE PUBLISHING and CROCE PUBLISHING
This arrangement © 2012 TIME IN A BOTTLE PUBLISHING and CROCE PUBLISHING
All Rights Controlled and Administered by EMI APRIL MUSIC INC.
All Rights Reserved International Copyright Secured Used by Permission

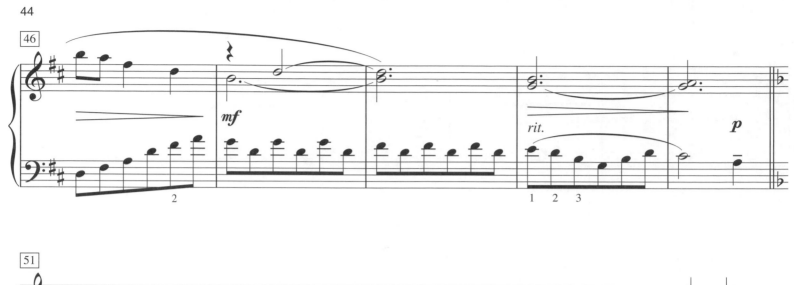

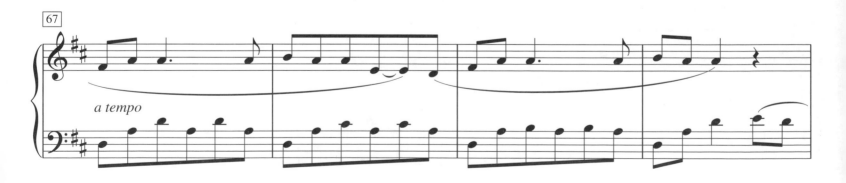

WHERE DO I BEGIN
(Love Theme)
from the Paramount Picture LOVE STORY

Words by CARL SIGMAN
Music by FRANCIS LAI
Arranged by Phillip Keveren

Copyright © 1970, 1971 Sony/ATV Music Publishing LLC
Copyright Renewed 1998, 1999 and Assigned to Sony/ATV Music Publishing LLC and Music Sales Corporation
This arrangement Copyright © 2012 Sony/ATV Music Publishing LLC and Music Sales Corporation
All Rights on behalf of Sony/ATV Music Publishing LLC Administered by Sony/ATV Music Publishing LLC, 8 Music Square West, Nashville, TN 37203
International Copyright Secured   All Rights Reserved